MISTY COPELAND

Ballet Dancer

Kaitlin Scirri

Cavendish Square

New York

Published in 2020 by Cavendish Square Publishing, LLC
243 5th Avenue, Suite 136, New York, NY 10016

First Edition

Website: cavendishsq.com

This publication represents the opinions and views of the author based on his or her personal experience, knowledge, and research. The information in this book serves as a general guide only. The author and publisher have used their best efforts in preparing this book and disclaim liability rising directly or indirectly from the use and application of this book.

All websites were available and accurate when this book was sent to press.

Library of Congress Cataloging-in-Publication Data

Names: Scirri, Kaitlin author.
Title: Misty Copeland : ballet dancer / Kaitlin Scirri.
Description: First Edition. | New York : Cavendish Square, 2020. |
Series: Barrier-Breaker bios | Audience: Grade level for this book is grades 1-4. |
Includes webography. | Includes bibliographical references and index.
Identifiers: LCCN 2019010764 (print) | LCCN 2019014506 (ebook) |
ISBN 9781502649638 (ebook) | ISBN 9781502649621(library bound) |
ISBN 9781502649607 (pbk.) | ISBN 9781502649614 (6 pack)
Subjects: LCSH: Copeland, Misty--Juvenile literature. | Ballet dancers--United States--Biography--
Juvenile literature. | African American dancers--Biography--Juvenile literature.
Classification: LCC GV1785.C635 (ebook) | LCC GV1785.C635 S35 2020 (print) | DDC 792.0892--dc23
LC record available at https://lccn.loc.gov/2019010764

Editor: Alexis David
Copy Editor: Nathan Heidelberger
Associate Art Director: Alan Sliwinski
Designer: Christina Shults
Production Coordinator: Karol Szymczuk
Photo Research: J8 Media

Printed in the United States of America

TABLE OF CONTENTS

Misty Copeland is seen here dancing in a ballet in 2015.

CHAPTER 1

WHO IS MISTY COPELAND?

Misty Copeland is a ballerina. Ballerinas dance on their toes in a style of dance called **ballet**. In the past, ballerinas were mostly white, but Misty Copeland is black. In 2015, she became the first African American woman to be a lead dancer for a ballet company called the American Ballet Theatre (ABT).

EARLY LIFE

Misty Copeland was born in 1982. Her family didn't have much money. They moved into a motel room. Copeland lived with her mother, stepfather, brothers, and sisters.

FINDING BALLET

Copeland liked to dance. She started ballet classes at age thirteen. Copeland followed her teacher's movements. The other girls had years of training, but Copeland learned faster than them. Her teacher knew she was special.

FAST FACT

At first, Copeland couldn't pay for ballet clothes. She took her first class in shorts, a T-shirt, and gym socks.

Copeland, shown here at age sixteen, practiced for hours in dance studios like the one seen here.

Copeland didn't have money for more classes. Her teacher helped her. She gave Copeland a **scholarship**. Her teacher also paid for her special dance clothes.

PRACTICE MAKES PERFECT

Copeland is seen here with Olu Evans.

Misty Copeland joined the American Ballet Theatre's main group in 2001. She was given many parts, but she wanted different parts. Copeland was shy. She was too nervous to ask for different parts. She practiced asking. Copeland practiced with a friend named Olu Evans. He helped her practice what to say. Then, Copeland talked to her director. She asked for different parts. Her practice worked! She was given new parts to dance.

At first, Copeland thought ballet was boring. After some time, though, she began to love ballet. She was invited to special schools just for dancers. She kept practicing and working hard.

BECOMING A BALLERINA

In 2015, Copeland became a **principal dancer** for ABT. Copeland broke a **barrier** when she did this. No black ballerina had been a principal dancer for ABT before. Copeland showed that people of all races could be ballerinas.

FAST FACT

Ballerinas dance on their toes. It often takes years of training. Copeland learned in just three months!

This Barbie doll was made to look like Misty Copeland in one of her ballet costumes.

CHAPTER 2

BREAKING BARRIERS

Misty Copeland learned ballet quickly, but it was very hard work. Copeland practiced many hours a day. Sometimes she danced for seven or eight hours. Dancing took up most of her time. She didn't have time with friends. She didn't see her family very much. However, she didn't stop working hard. She wanted to be a ballerina.

Copeland is shown here stretching in a dance studio in 2017.

HARD WORK

Ballerinas sometimes get hurt while dancing. They might jump and land hard. They might break a bone. Sometimes they pull or hurt their muscles. In 2001, Copeland hurt her back while dancing. It was a bad

Copeland has worn many different costumes as a ballerina.

injury. It took a long time to heal. Copeland was nineteen. She had just started dancing with her ballet company's main group. She had to take a whole year off to heal. Copeland was very sad, but she didn't give up. She let her back heal. Then, she went back to practicing and dancing.

Copeland often dances with male partners on stage.

STANDING OUT

Copeland faced problems when she went back to dancing. She didn't look like the other ballerinas. Most ballerinas were very thin. Copeland had a curvy body. Copeland's dance teachers wanted her to change. They wanted her to lose weight and look like the other ballerinas in her company.

FAST FACT

Misty Copeland trained so hard that her feet would hurt. She soaked them in ice to make them feel better.

Copeland didn't give in. She learned exercises to make her body strong. She also learned about healthy foods. Copeland learned to take care of herself and to **accept** herself. That means she learned to love her body the way it was. Her teachers saw that she accepted her body. They began to accept it too. They stopped telling her to lose weight.

Copeland's skin color also made her different. Most ballerinas were white. Copeland was black. Copeland danced like the other ballerinas, but her skin color made her stand out on stage. Some people called her a distraction. A distraction is someone who takes attention away from someone else. Copeland had to make herself blend in. Sometimes, she even had to paint herself white. However, she was proud of her skin color. She learned not to listen to people who said mean things about her. She kept working hard to become a great ballerina.

SOLOIST

At first, Copeland danced in a group. In 2007, Copeland became a **soloist**. A soloist gets to dance alone on stage. A soloist stands out from the other dancers. Copeland was only the third African

FAST FACT

Misty Copeland danced in the 2018 Disney film *The Nutcracker and the Four Realms*. She played the Ballerina Princess.

Copeland is shown here at an event for *The Nutcracker and the Four Realms*.

BEING BRAVE

Growing up, Misty Copeland was different from her friends. Her friends lived in houses. Copeland lived in a motel room. Her family was poor. Her mother worked many jobs to put food on the table. Copeland was embarrassed, but she learned to be brave. She danced to forget her problems. Years later, Copeland was different again. She looked different from the other ballerinas. However, Copeland was used to being different. She didn't run away. She was brave again. She faced her problems. She stood up for herself. She didn't quit. She became a lead ballerina.

American female soloist in her ballet company's history. Copeland was proud of herself.

PRINCIPAL DANCER

In 2015, Copeland became a principal dancer. A principal dancer is the star of the show. Copeland was the first African American woman to become a principal dancer with her ballet company. Her hard work had paid off. Copeland's dream had come true! She is now a role model. A role model is someone others can look up to.

Misty Copeland wrote a children's book about becoming a ballerina.

Copeland, seen here in 2014, is a role model for other dancers.

CHAPTER 3

CHANGING THE FACE OF BALLET

Misty Copeland has changed ballet. She has broken a barrier for African American dancers. She uses her talent and fame to help other dancers.

ROLE MODEL

Copeland is a role model for girls and women. She teaches them to love themselves and their bodies. In 2017, Copeland wrote a health book. It's called *Ballerina Body*. The book teaches women how to

Misty Copeland wrote a book called *Life in Motion*.

be healthy and strong. Copeland has also written about her life. In 2014, she wrote a book about her struggles. It's called *Life in Motion*. Copeland hopes to set an example for others.

RAISING AWARENESS

Ballerinas need special shoes and tights. Ballet shoes are most often light pink and are worn with white or light pink tights. Copeland needed darker shoes and tights. She needed them to match her skin color, but no one made dark ballet shoes for African American dancers. Copeland had to paint her shoes. Copeland has shown that black ballerinas need ballet shoes and clothes that look good with their skin color just like white ballerinas do. Copeland has raised awareness. Raising awareness means she has taught people something. Now clothing companies make different kinds of ballet clothes and shoes. There are now different colors of tights and shoes to match different skin colors.

HELPING OTHERS

Many people helped Copeland become a ballerina. Now she likes to help others. In 2013, Copeland helped her ballet company with a special project called Project Plié. A **plié** is a ballet movement.

BRAVE BALLERINAS

Misty Copeland wasn't the first African American ballerina. Raven Wilkinson was an African American ballerina in the 1950s. She joined a ballet company, but she had to pretend to be a white ballerina. She had to paint her face white. Wilkinson's struggle made a path for Copeland. Now Copeland's struggle has made a path for new ballerinas. Wilkinson was a teacher and friend to Copeland. Wilkinson and Copeland made a film together. They wanted to inspire future ballerinas of all races. They share their stories in the film. It's called *A Ballerina's Tale*.

Misty Copeland has paved the way for ballerinas of all races.

Misty Copeland thinks social media is fun. She shares the world of ballet with her fans. She uses Facebook, Twitter, and Instagram.

Project Plié works with the Boys and Girls Clubs of America. Copeland took her first ballet classes at one of these clubs.

Project Plié helps bring ballet to kids in many communities. A community is a place where people live. Through Project Plié, kids can learn about dance. They can take lessons. They can even win scholarships to help pay for ballet training.

Copeland, seen here in 2014, works to bring ballet to communities all over the United States.

TIMELINE

1982 Misty Copeland is born in Kansas City, Missouri.

1996 Copeland begins her ballet training.

2001 Copeland becomes a dancer in the main company of the American Ballet Theatre (ABT).

2007 Copeland becomes the third African American female soloist in ABT history.

2013 Copeland helps create Project Plié to bring ballet to different communities.

2015 Copeland becomes the first African American female principal dancer at the ABT.

2018 Copeland is part of Disney's movie *The Nutcracker and the Four Realms*.

GLOSSARY

accept To be happy with something the way it is, without trying to change it.

ballet A type of dance that tells a story through careful steps and movements.

barrier Something that blocks or stops someone from doing something.

plié A dance movement that involves bending the knees.

principal dancer The first, or lead, dancer in a show.

scholarship Money to help pay for school or lessons.

soloist Someone who dances alone on stage, away from everyone else.

FIND OUT MORE

BOOKS

Isbell, Hannah. *Misty Copeland: Ballerina*. New York, NY: Enslow Publishing, 2017.

Lyons, Kelly Starling. *A Girl Named Misty: The True Story of Misty Copeland*. New York, NY: Scholastic, 2018.

WEBSITE

The Official Website of Misty Copeland

https://mistycopeland.com

VIDEO

Under Armour Ad: I Will What I Want

https://youtu.be/zWJ5_HiKhNg

INDEX

Page numbers in **boldface** refer to images. Entries in **boldface** are glossary terms.

ABOUT THE AUTHOR

Kaitlin Scirri is a freelance editor and author of books for children and teens. She holds a bachelor's degree in writing from the State University of New York at Buffalo State College. Other titles by Scirri include *Civic Values: Property Rights*, *The Science of Superpowers: Controlling Electricity and Weather*, *The Science of Superpowers: Invisibility and X-Ray Vision*, and *Inventions That Changed the World: How Facebook Changed the World*. A fan of ballet, Scirri enjoys Copeland's dancing and thoroughly enjoyed sharing her story.